July 2005

To Kit— Every stream and every mountain stops when it enters a lake... Love Joe

Vents

Joseph Zaccardi

Joseph Zaccardi

Acknowledgements:

BLUE UNICORN: "The Yellow Emperor."
POET LORE: "Rings."
RUNES: "Listen." CLOUD VIEW POETS: "Body of War."
THE SEATTLE REVIEW; MARIN POETRY CENTER
ANTHOLOGY VOL. VII: "Enlisting," Listening."
PASSAGER: "Mekong Delta 1967,"
"A Lay Of Feathers 1975."
THE BALTIMORE REVIEW: "Peach Hotel."
THE BARNABE MOUNTAIN REVIEW; POETS
AGAINST THE WAR: "Search And Rescue."

Special thanks to Serina Bardell, Dave Eng, C. B. Follett,
Margaret Kaufman and Susan Terris.

My heartfelt gratitude to Mary Golding for her
meticulous and unflagging help with this manuscript.

This book is made possible by a grant from the
Marin Arts Council.

Cover Design: Jennifer Ryan Wilde, chaotech design.

Cover Art/Frontispiece: Patrick Smith, "Post Verdict."
© 1995 pancakepress.com.

Additional copies available from www.pancakepress.com.

ISBN: 09762478-0-1
Special Edition.

CONTENTS

RETURNING   67

ENLISTING

THE HERE AND NOW

I live with a lifetime of dead friends,
loved ones, a few I don't even miss.
The past always harangues.
I avoid tarot readers and seers.
What lies there? catastrophes,
winning lottery tickets (don't bet on it),
a handful of really good meals, months of boring parties.
Put the future off to the last possible second, I say.
A voice from the other side calls, telegram
for mister so and so.

                  Reluctantly I answer.
More wires from the dearly departed.
My hands grow busy shuffling cards
from the western union of yin and yang.
Try reading the blocked letters:
MUST TALK TO YOU   STOP
CAN'T REST IN PEACE   END STOP
I tell you, I won't talk to them,
the dead ones; but they call on
the unusual, use brain waves,
heavenly connections.

                  I cut the deck,
it's my father telling me again,
certificates of deposit are better than equities.
He should know, he's a futures' inside trader
who can't resist reminding me
I'm the son of a dead man. Christ,
I want to say, but that leads to a whole
other paradox. I fan cards out on green felt,
choose the Two of Diamonds (my dead sister),
put her under my pillow, listen to child-talk.

LISTENING

She tells me they would unstitch their clothes,
resew them with the inside out. She tells me
I couldn't know, can't understand; bread so hard
soaking it in bitter coffee didn't help. All this
because I said the crusty ends are best.
If you are pampered all your life, she says,
everything given to you, then yes, the ends
are better, and if you could have any fine coat,
any silk scarf, then yes, you could treasure
a worn pair of dungarees with patched holes.
She tells me they lived in tents, boiled bed linens,
shared bath water, doctored their own illnesses,
fed a scrawny chicken night crawlers and waited,
yes– it's different when you have a house, a roof
over your head, then camping out, missing out,
doing without is fun. She tells me I don't know.
I listen, nod, heard it all before. She gets impatient,
not angry. Sure it's fine when you have... Here,
eat this last piece of cheese, think of it as the last
piece you'll have. She hopes I'll never have
to know what it was like. Yes, she says, it's better
not to know.

DANCE OF THE TAI CHI MASTERS

San Francisco

Holding a small red book above his head,
he stands on a round pedestal

on Stockton Street in Chinatown
juggling his Mandarin with bits of English.

"Mr. Englishman," "Imperialist," he rambles,
red banners, gold characters circling him.

There is always a knot of shoppers
around him vying over bins of foo kwa, bok choy, gai lon.

A chicken escapes from one of many wire cages
stacked at the curb; the farmer steps

on the wing, grabs hold of the feet, hands shoot
out to buy her and she is gone

in the time it takes to feel nothing.
I am distracted by my own thoughts.

Smells of dim sum come
from the Golden Dragon restaurant.

Holding a small red book above his head
he looks as though he's directing a tangle of traffic.

Neither I nor the Toishan nor Cantonese immigrants
understand his Mandarin.

A pretty Chinese girl sticks her fingers
into the gills of a rock cod

and I'm out of breath, lost
as I turn uphill, the sounds behind me

like bells. On a balcony
a Tai Chi master moves

to strings of Stravinsky's
Le Sacre du Printemps.

Tonight I will sleep with all my windows open,
there is so much I need

to give up
to the air.

THE YELLOW EMPEROR

Twenty-five hundred years before Jesus,
Huang-Ti sat among the ginkgo
breathing in the brevity of their color.
He waited out the day and wrote about the stars,
meditated on jasmine, lingering.
The night sky was overcast,
the stars invisible
but he knew long after his death
people would be bewildered
if he didn't mention stars.
About the quiet smell of jasmine
he wrote nothing,
he needed to leave out the fragrance
to fill in his poem
with silence.

TOUCHING

I sail with an old man who tacks
from the Sea of Cortez against
the wind toward the Pacific. I yell
in his ear, Where is it we're heading?
There, the horizon, he calls back.
And before I can complain
he pulls a rainbow from his creel.
What he says afterwards and where
we sail I cannot tell you
but I know we keep to our course.

A thousand miles north in a city,
a woman lies on a sidewalk,
the front page of a daily newspaper
between her and her bed.
It is her possession of words.
She is still, and disturbs no one.

And on Kehoe Beach, a boy
of seven finds a starfish;
crouching, he lowers his head
and turns an ear close without touching.
What are you doing, I ask.
Listening, he replies. And what
do you hear? I don't know yet.
I've never heard anything like it,
and I'm afraid it's alive.

TO SU TUNG-PO

It's not quite noon and I'm already drunk,
the wine bottle empty as my soul. It is you,
Su Tung-po, I think of; dressing to go out,
a walk in the woods. I do the same, avoid
the sea. No water can sate me this time.
The trees make a path to follow. My legs
weaken, and too soon to quiet myself I stop
and watch Mayflies, and the unseeable, caress
blooms of a buckeye. Everything seems natural
and unexplainable, like lumbering clouds
going nowhere, coming from nowhere.
I think of your spinning girls (silkworms)
and the sweet smell in the village
of cocoons boiling. But this is a dead end,
wasting thoughts on a day already devoid,
the unknown. What haunts me
is different. What hell a landscape is,
how frightening trees can be, filled
and emptied, like this too long day.

IN A FOREST

Space is meaning.

Trees crowd the view.
The bells of wild onion become the snow
of mountain ranges, my falling step
the thrum of thunder, breath the impending
storm. And all dark gathering finds
a path down, settles on outstretched limbs
and palm-up leaves. The sun gives
in to its colors; the dimming, the shades.
This world of compromise.

Time is a task.

Why, Master, does the forest give way
to roads? Silence is the reply. I listen
to a car approaching, the tick
the tires make over the macadam's
cracks and seams. What choice do we have?
giant dwarfed by forest, forest by roads.

FLIGHT

The morning is so warm
a fly trapped at the window pane
lies on its side. Alive,
but resigned
to a predictable,
indistinguishable death.

I dress, almost slow dance into dark
suit, shoes and tie
to attend the funeral of a friend
wasted from the racking, coughing,
shivering. Taken away.

At Luther's church, I am
unapproachable. An understated
presence banging at the door.
We bury, give back
in ritual ancient grief.
I want to feel comfort here.
Try to say I held this man's hand.
Instead, feel nothing.

At home I open the window
to free the stuffy interior
of myself.
My graceful fly corpse
wings up and banks
toward the black oak. Out of sight.
My heart beating in place.

18

KALI

It is morning   Light is air
Thin through banyan   thick

on plumeria   orange   yellow
ripening on the tops

                              I saw
you from across the room
the night before   at the noodle shop

                                        Steam
from clay bowls of udon   ramen
Cold soba in pottery

I heard you say your name   Halley

Like the comet named for the blue
on black light

                                        Waking
you said Kali   drawing the K
with imaginary chopsticks

                              Lips
touching lips   Tasting

                              the rise of morning
from the first time
it ever rose

ENLISTING

There was this form to fill out, though
I think it was more questionnaire. It had
the force of law on its side, at the end
we would all sign, and there was
a warning about perjury, explicit.
And implied was something different,
something like: You will fill this out,
answer true or false, no matter whether
it is true or false. There were questions
of conscience, of objection: Do you
believe in war: True. Do you object
to killing: False. Are you a sissy, have you
ever known one, played around... (though
they used a bigger word, a forceful word
loaded with arms, commands, orders)
and we all put down: No. Perhaps
we all knew someone, even ourselves.
Maybe this couldn't be but we all
signed and took our clothes off, cut
our hair down, swore an oath, and
some of us went to the fighting, some
of us came back, some didn't.
We were lied to, and we lied back.

PEACH HOTEL

Paul McCartney was singing "Hey Jude."
The Kaohsiung bar girl rubbed my thigh
and said in a crisp British accent,
"Buy me another drink."
She laughed at the cold tea,
pretending it was Kentucky bourbon.
I loved her for that, and desired
what any twenty-year-old desires:
to touch anyplace, to reach anywhere.
At the Peach Hotel we quickly undressed,
fumbling with each other.
Our passion a cruel closeness.
From the street below, firecrackers
dispelled any calm we might have felt,
their noise lightened the sky.
Busy merchants hailed passersby
enticing them with descriptions
of fresh fish, aphrodisiacs, quality of oranges.
The smell of gunpowder,
ghosting a labyrinth of shades,
greeted the lunar new year.
Children gobbled moon cakes. Eyes still,
holding flares against the sky.
Together in the shadow of our room
our bodies trembled,
her tears touched my arm
leaving pale scars.

BODY OF WAR

I remember a flower floating on water. What do I call
 it?
White blossom swimming in place? Brother holding
 brother?

To stanch bleeding apply gauze and pressure,
 then bandage.
I remember trawlers. Lean brown men. Nets laid in
 the brine

like fine doilies. Where red tide meets blue, sister
 caressing sister.
If there's a wound to the abdomen, inject morphine,
 tell them

it doesn't look bad, you've seen worse and theirs looks
 good,
pretty good. I remember gathering this part to fit that
 part. How

can I tell you? That it didn't bother me? There was no
 time to think?
That it was just a bad dream? Some nights I lie in bed
 trembling,

and if I try to speak, only consonant sounds come out,
 words
without vowels. Arm without "a." Leg without "e."
 And head.

How do I say head?

MEKONG DELTA 1967

An overlay of feathers
reflected in the dark water.

Vague slivers of dreams play over my eyelids,
fanning this last vestige of sleep.

I drift toward a thatched village
where an old man dangles his long beard,

dripping in the last light of stars
after his lonely swim,

mouth gulping black air.
A carp trails its kite tail,

takes refuge in coral reefs;
a place of cold blue light.

A cool hand slips under the back of my neck
to the time my sister drowned.

Fish belly white, life taken
by a different body of water.

I start inventing pictures—
she flies multi-colored scarves,

leaps free, weightless in the sun
casting long shadows over fallen pine cones.

I awake to distant sounds
of discovery.

Angels of war swoop
to rescue me.

As the helicopter beats its wings,
I can speak no words, only watch.

LISTEN

I will tell you a memory   something barely left
just tatters   a fringe of soft strings
It lies nine thousand miles   from here
where I lay on tatami   unclothed in the warm night...
bits and pieces filled with sleep   and dreams...
This near   so far...
He covered my body   with his body
his scent   sandalwood
and whispered   "I have found you"
Promised   he would do everything
There is so little   left...
oh yes— his lips   I remember his lips
they tasted of spice   clove and cardamom.

SEARCH AND RESCUE

In my journal I write: Rescue.
Today we set out to rescue men
from an LST
run aground in the waters off the
Mekong.
We are not a part of this country.

The first thing I notice is the
whistle
of bullets through leaves, like birds
tearing bits apart.
What are the names of these trees.

The body we find is stripped of
flesh, eyelids
peeled away.
The body is blue and bloated.
It stares at us.
There are no birds in the trees, only rain.

We taste the metal of rain, look
into that face.
Indecent, red curl around glutinous
eyes.
We force ourselves to look at the
hairless
engorged genitals.
Is he one of ours or one of theirs.

Everything about the rescue
is disproportionate. Everything
about the rise
and cry above, pornographic. The
choking roar.
The cover of tracer and fire.

White blooms at the cross of two
rivers.
Helicopters e-vac us to our ship.
Breath
smoking in the reefers. We store
and tag the body.

The sun is brown over the hot
jungle.
I vomit into the cold shaft of the
pallet lift.
Everything until now is a lie.

MEMORIAL DAY

There's so much in the sky:
gods of course, angry fathers,
magicians, nymphs,
and a cat scratching white
claw marks across it all,
courtesy of the Blue Angels.
The noise. The racket.
Banging, clattering,
everyone in the mood
to remodel, repair, replace
an old screendoor, re-cane a chair.
And it isn't even summer,
yet smoke from barbecues
carries smells of charred meats
and drumsticks. Some people
(children? they all look small
from my perch of a house)
are flying kites, if only
they'd get out of the way.
Wind hushes this day, reminds
me of past battles; the waving
arms of those below seeking
rescue. Today a day of memory.
Darkness covers for tomorrow:
Tomorrow is the invisible
silence of air.

A LAY OF FEATHERS 1975

Where I enter the foyer,
a bouquet of peacock feathers arranged
in an imitation Ming vase— freestanding.
A sensual party well underway,
gurus blowing grass, speed freaks in slo-mo,
brownies made with hash—
food, booze and young girls, pretty boys— I feel stripped,
naked as a Pontiac Indian without headdress—
the smell of turkey wafting from the kitchen.
These are heady days— all of us dazed from a long-fought
war for nothing. But this is not the family holiday
(not a pilgrim within 9000 miles), this is April 30,
official end of the war in Nam.
Someone lights a bong,
the initial blast of flame is napalm,
and then the feathers fall away...

CALLING ALABAMA

It's midnight here on the west coast. Ten more days
  to go before 1999 starts
    to sound old fashioned.

I pace the living room, looking up and down the walls,
  I touch, no, caress my hornbill
    from the Ivory Coast,

phone an old friend from boot camp. It's later there
  but he doesn't mind, in fact sounds relieved
    like he's put off something dangerous.

We start talking about our youth, when over the hill
  meant AWOL, laughing about
    the good times

we had, when getting drunk and sick was fun. Before
  you know it we're blubbering, two grown men
    bawling our eyes out,

over the first time I had grits, (I'm a Yankee and don't
  know grits from farina)
    and he's losing it, I'm losing it.

And New Year's Eve is looming, like that black wall
  in DC. All those names staring
    back,

lost in the ground. It's getting darker here and lighter
  in Alabama. Good talking to you good buddy
    we both say, hang up.

I get a tall glass of milk and some oatmeal cookies,
  and look out at the largest
    full moon in 134 years,

first night of winter, and he's probably watching the first
  rays of the new sun, holding
    his Purple Heart next to his heart,

smiling just a little, saying it'll be all right, yeah all right.
  It's what men do
    for other men

at some terrible hour. I see something moving in the brush
  on the downside
    of my yard.

It lets out a horrible scream, one that freezes me under
  the white circle of light
    over the kitchen table.

Ron didn't put the .45 back in the writing desk drawer.
  It would be three months
    before I found out.

I think when he put the muzzle in his mouth, a train
  whispered through
    the Appalachian Valley,

then wailed long and hard, as if to say, look, my spiral
  of white smoke will join
    the purple.

LIU CHING-WEN REPLIES
TO SU TUNG-PO

It is Dragon Festival here in Hangchow.
Teachers show their students how to fashion
rice paper into toy boats, how to wax the skin,
giving each a candle to place in the bow.
At dusk fireflies along the Grand Canal.
Children light their tapers; a line of miniature
sampans journeying like a fleet of citrons
into the bay, and as they seem to stall,
flicker out, the stars take over. Not once
in my long life has one come back.
All gone away, yet always with me.
A lesson we teach our children.
The end is the same as the beginning.
You say you'd have me remember
the good sights. This is one.

ECHO

Each call insistent, each reply (one thousand one)
comes back altered. Silence in between.
A cavernous recall of the empty, a gaping invitation,
and then another riposte (one thousand two)
of something akin to lightning, the charge
of a subtle change in time. Time a second time.
(One thousand three). It's a kind of play with
the hoped for answer, the roll. Thunder
of perception, thought quicker than the split,
the splice of light and sound. A voice raised
high in the sky (one thousand four) ready
to strike a deal, make a trade.

LOVING

I KNEW ONCE

There was the man with the green
wooden leg, made up to keep us kids
from wandering too far into the woods.
And Ruth kissing me in the schoolyard,
then Francis Kratzerfish told Mrs. Heck,
our second grade teacher, about it.
My best friends Victor (who swallowed
a half dollar) and Michael, two
twelve year olds, erupting with shouts,
wild boys riding English Racers.
And a carload of teenagers with fake ID's
crossing the Verrazano-Narrows Bridge
to drink draught Schaefer's in Brooklyn.
Walks in the Village among the mysterious.
And in Kamakura, 1969, with Fumiko
at the Buddha, her skin soapstone
fading now— the first person
I touched honestly.

HOLDING HANDS

at midnight or lyrics like that
but this is the beginning of the weekend;
Happy Hour at Perry's on a Friday.
Someone's yelling at the TV set because
a giant of a man drops a ball, misses the net—
was he fouled? Big crowd tonight, one bar
stool empty and this ordinary looking guy
comes in and takes it. The bartender,
a stunning woman, shiny hair tied back,
says, what'll it be? And he covers her
hand with his— for a moment it's too quiet
to be awake— she doesn't flinch,
maintains eye contact, there's
an equilibrium here, a mutual sedative.
He orders a JB and soda and when
she turns away, he smells his hand—
now don't get the wrong idea, don't jump
to conclusions, we have a way to go yet.
Watch her, she touches her fingertips
to her lips, lightly, briefly, before pouring
scotch over ice. It's then, when music
in the background clears the air with words,
the song pleasantly unconstricted, clearly says,
"nice work if you can get it and you can get it..."

ISLAND

Two weeks before she told me,
we packed a picnic lunch
and went to Angel Island.

She had been diagnosed with MS.

We spread a blanket on crisp eucalyptus,
ate cold chicken,
drank sweet wine.

It's the slow kind, she told me.

We lay back watching the sway of long leaves
and made love while sail boats
plied white-capped swells.

It's the good kind, she told me.

This is the news
we shared, our hearts brutalized.
Two weeks after Angel Island.

CELESTIAL

A river of ants climbs up the trunk of a
peach tree into the cover of leaves.

I run my fingers over a photo of you
from our yearbook. Under your name

it says, "Most likely to love." It says,
"You dare to penetrate the stars."

The four-cornered hat with tassel
sits square on your head; an astronomer

looking at the nine dead moons of Jupiter.
I remember looking at your feet

the night of graduation, we were drunk,
we were weightless in our gravity, our ominous

beauty. You held me like the high notes
on an airless planet, so long it hurts still,

the way ants hurt a peach. From the inside
having their way with the heart.

USING DISCRETION

Sitting with a woman on the edge of an unmade bed;
light slips through the bay window.
It is nine hours into her birthday.
She smokes a cigarette cowboy style.
She is of course naked, sexy as hell.
I tell myself to get up. Saying I have to go
back to the other side of the lightwell;
my apartment empty except for undone dishes,
a dying sword fern,
a new copy of Raymond Carver's
"Ultramarine."

She says, don't go yet.
There is anguish about her.
We go to the shower,
I bathe her with loofa and bubbles,
she twists and cries.
Because she is happy?
Later, we lie down, hold each other.
I feel guilty; say I am sorry but don't mean it.
She asks me to leave, quietly.

It is like pulling myself out of myself.
She closes the door.
Her husband returns the next day.
He's carrying boxes of gifts;
lets them tumble
to the floor.
Hangs onto her.
I'm afraid to look across.
Afraid to breathe.
Afraid the glass may fly
into a thousand pieces.

THERE ARE NO STARS

The sky is a shadow box, a night in overcoat.
Because it is summer,
honeysuckle in bloom, in a stitch
of celestial perfection,
I hold a jar of lightning bugs, fingertips tapping
thunder on the tin lid.
In the sky there's a nimbus, a woman's
shoulder, long black hair.
The night creeps in nothing, a cricket speaks,
stars in black absence.
I remember watching meteors drop through
a dark horizon, I remember
their movable beauty, I think it is always winter
where they are, waiting
to pierce the summer, as I unleash the captive
sound of a bell.

THE TRYST

Late spring. Outside, the mountain ash
berry in bright-red clusters. I bring you
a mimosa, mistakenly calling it a "miasma."

You laugh, correct me, and with the slightest
touch I show you how the leaves quickly fold,
close in. You grill a chateaubriand with shallots,

sake— and maybe because you drink one
too many glasses of white wine or
because you like bad puns you call it

"chapeaubriand." How can we not take
what is given, never twist it to suit
our own desires?

FROM THE CITY OF LIGHT

Remember when we picked sand dollars
        at low tide on Stinson?

the unspendable.

It's been too many years, the space
        between our touches grows.

Now I'm back

on the lookout, and you?
        somewhere on another grid?

I could walk

and never leave an imprint,
        never re-find you.

Thank God for postcards;
        it's a strange time-saving device.

Ondaatje says

they're the American equivalent of the sonnet.
        I'm tempted to write

what I feel... what I count on...

but it's the waves I'm counting backwards,
        the receding.

My slow scrawl turning up

the side of the card wishing
        you were here.

Or warped back to a seamless beach.

POSTCARD

Sitting outside the Cafe Trieste
I am watching the neon lights on Columbus Avenue,
when two teenagers, about age thirteen,
probably on their first date, walk by my table—
a moment and there I am staring,
a slight smile lifting my lips.
A few steps past they start to giggle
and the young woman, new to admiration
turns her head and blows me a kiss, not unkindly.
At that instant all the traffic lights blink amber
(something to do with a relay switch overload)
and the boy gives her new breasts a quick look.
When I think back on moments of beauty,
I remember this date, this night, this light.

STRAWBERRY CREPE

The rough plank floors
cried when you walked
about the kitchen.
And on one side of the stove
was a compartment
for burning wood,
floating warm air.
You explained:
the first crepe was always bad,
like the first born.
Your mother had said this to you.
I wanted to scoop up
your mangled perfection.
Eat it with the hunger I felt,
so that we might recognize each other.
Communicate the way sunlight
loves what it touches.

The call came at 5AM,
the jangle of rings saying
you had killed yourself.
The old O'Keefe & Merritt's
gas valves turned on.
You sought shelter in there,
trembling in the dark enamel cavern.
In the seconds after you were gone
the electric streetcar hissed,
its hydraulic brakes
smelling of ozone.
And I heard you say:
The true fruit of the strawberry
is in the small seeds.

WATERBORNE

When I say, I can see clear to the bottom,
don't think of the invisible. Think of the visible,
turquoise surface, the white sand below,
shimmer of sunfish, stir of current. When
I say transparent, it's not that I can see
through you. It is more into. In water
we become what the water feels, the way
salt unites to our skin, the way an angelfish
kisses the shell of a conch and backs away.
Each touch permanent. Untied.

A WALK IN THE PARK

Under the out-of-place palms planted
side by side along the promenade, a Sunday,
the balm of Easter, Passover, the mystic phase,
Goddess of Spring in a breeze-blown silence,
and the eyes of wiseguys watch wistfully.
She wears white, a chemise, and pays no attention,
leaving in her wake erect penises and itchy testicles,
heaving bosoms and wet vaginas.
Men go mad for lack of kisses and women
flicking fans hyperventilate. It's such an unfair time:
blooms profuse, spring sun perfect, tiny
wrens flitting about, to hear them chirping
is to know desire. Day passes into powdery lights,
night cools, the tempest temporized— The self-sated,
even the unsated, breathe a breath like a flood
when gates of dams are opened.
And all around we hear the stars laughing.

WHAT IS BEST WE LEAVE

Ruby plumeria on Kauai,
mornings at sea,
your grip on the ship's rail
as though it is
a life preserver.

Morning walks
on Waimea, sand cool,
the bare beautiful
nature of things;
folding our hands
each in the other.

Year by year
we gather shells,
store spectacular views
on postcards,

collect salt,
polish memories
into fine
marble.

Desire growing stronger
as the body lessens.

AFTER THE MOVIE

we pick up a bouquet of wisteria,
talk about the Victorian Painted Ladies,
how Edwardians would be more suited
to this neighborhood, less pretentious.
Your apartment is filled
with Indonesian art,
windows decorated
with carved beads of monkeypod.
You take off your shirt and tie,
your white tank top,
put on music by Rodrigo,
talk about the guy at the office
you have a crush on.
I pretend I don't care,
stretch out on the divan,
count on my fingertips
the 8th notes
of the classical guitarist—
that's when you lean over,
kiss me on the lips.

THE JOURNEY

I believe in transformations, and that nothing
changes. The worm lazing in the unfinished.
Yesterday turns on the ground into ground.
The cores of apple melt in the aging, desire
ripens, sweetens the soil with its loss.
Pie in the sky? Old friend, hope unearths me.
Steel forks on the working end churn
the living with more living. Larvae uncovered
to light, glisten. And above? I watch
migration in return.

LIGHT SPEED

We are walking around the Lagunitas reservoir,
two conversations going on, nothing verbal,
just the hard nouns of thought. The not far off
opposing shore expanding as we follow
the lake's course, and what at first seems nearer,
becomes more distant with change. A parallel universe,
land's edge looking up at the land's edge,
everything shifting, rippling the sleeves of time,
like putting a shirt on, hands entering a wormhole
of fabric and exiting (existing) in another place,
stretching, retracting, the fingers flicking off lint,
a loose thread. I recall a small article I saved
about researchers slowing light to a dead stop,
holding it in stasis, then releasing light
as an ordinary material particle, letting it go.
I turn to my traveling companion who has stopped,
we listen to a flotilla of dragonflies, their airborne sound
nearly imperceptible in our quiet, but they move
quickly away from us, the spell broken,
the earth once again flat, almost graspable.

LONELINESS

Landscape is a kind of lying,
mountains a kind of hope
against the flat fates.
The sky is a blue stone
gone gray, the sun a too-bright
seething liquid.
We think we're safe because
there are so many people, because
mountains are rock, the seas pliable—
we forget the scholars of Pompeii,
who etched on tablets of marble,
 "...placate the gods with sacrifice,"
encased now in lava, a topography
of embrace.
                    I say

among the crowds of people,
it is your unending absence
that hurts the most.

THE GIVING

There is no honor in being truthful
if it hurts someone; worse if you know
it will. There is grief in breaking a heart,
even if it is sledge-hammered down
to the finest silica— oh heart of stone—
it will not pass through the hourglass.
Time becomes the wound.
There is no courage in lying, even as
the changing color of leaves shades
the true nature of being. I have wished
harm on others, made use of that big
German word, taking satisfaction
in their failures. For this reason
I have banished myself to a cell
where I scrub at black mold and decay,
knowing full well it cannot be done.
This is a lesson I've learned;
I pass it along like a clean slate.

SOME LATE LINES

Waiting
for a meteor to shoot by,
watching old configurations,
I pace the L-shaped deck, note
the sounds my soles make,
listen in at the dark places
around trees, along fence line
and privacy wall. Someone
passes by out front, headlights
mooning the blacktop, and
a garbage truck moans
blocks away with its haul.
I remember a trout, fly-caught,
how it fought, and how good
it felt to let it go. It makes me
happy even now, stomach
tight from fasting,
sky motionless.

TRAVELING

A CHOICE OF DIRECTION

Driving 6 am until high noon,
like they say in the movies,
I came to a sign announcing I'd arrived.
On one corner a gas station and a diner
with chrome-colored eaves,
a chrome belt under its boxcar window.
Nothing on the other three corners,
the earth curving in all four directions
as though this is some important place
on the globe. It has the mystery
of something out of nowhere.
Like when I was ten and spun the whole earth,
each country a different color,
and stopped the spin with my index finger,
trying to imagine where I was, what it was like there.
Roy's diner, run by a family of Swedish descendants,
as though their covered wagon fell apart
at this spot and they settled here.
All the food— dogs, burgers, fried egg sandwiches—
comes with your choice of green or red chilies.
"What's the best road to take from here,"
I ask the waitress with gray flecks
in her long tied-back hair.
"The green chilies are hotter than the red chilies,"
she says, "this is your last chance
to fill your tank for the next 197 miles.
Everything on the menu is good."

Outside the wind blows from nowhere and everywhere.
Like someone trying to cool
a bowl of chili— problematic, seeing
as the green are hotter than the red.
I found the red are hot too.
Not often in life you get to choose
a road with no wrong decisions.
It's all symmetry and distance.
X marks the spot.
Four Corners.
A place I've been to,
a place to start out from.

ON HIGHWAY 902

past the salvage yard
where a '56 Buick
welded atop a 20' steel pole
advertises the obvious,
past the drive-in that shows
X-rated movies at midnight
and past the treeless
Christmas tree farm,
past Normal Square Hotel;
turning leaves of oak
on either side of me,
the sun hounding a horizon
noisy with red speed, listening
to Chuck Berry gravel
from the CD player, trying
to name something
without name, nail some thought
too fast to catch; I crest the road,
almost cream a family of wild turkey,
swerve, slow down,
check my rear view mirror—
they disappear in the drying weeds—
keep driving, both hands
on the wheel.

RINGS

Too much sound in the ear
can deafen the ear, too much light
in the eye can blind the eye.
What about voice? speaking in tongues?
What can damage hand signals?
How we survive is a phantom,
a trick of magic, a wave of a wand.
Strips of light and dark, bands of silver
we call day and night.
Each in our own way takes
what is offered as though from
an altar of giving and return.
Who is to say what is more beautiful,
the night or the day, sunset or sunrise;
one brings us hope for new beginnings,
one promises more to come after some rest.
Today I watch a boy in a wheelchair;
he unfurls, spins with bare hands
the spoked wheels, drawing
his own line of infinity, shuttling
his body on the busy sidewalk,
his hair spiked and jelled
in the fashion of a Mohawk,
his ears and lips pierced
with silver rings.

RIDE

Last time I took a bus cross-country
a man in the front row seat
was talking to the driver.
Long gnarled hands resting on his knees,
he leaned forward, careful not to
cross the yellow "Keep Back" line
on the aisle floor and said,
"This my last trip, going to stay
at my daughter's in Roseville.
Too old to live alone anymore.
See she needs my help. I'm handy,
can fix anything that's broke,
except a broke man," he laughed.
The driver's eyes flickered
in the rear view mirror as if to reassure
the rest of us that he was watching the road
and I saw him glance nervously up
at the "Don't Talk To Driver" warning.
He said to his friend, like they'd known
each other since childhood, "Ham,
why don't you call me when you settle in—
I'll come visit. You sit back, relax."
Now I'm on this bus thirty years later,
coming the other way, and I see the sign
for Roseville, but the bus doesn't stop,
just passes by. And I'm thinking
about what Ham said, how you can't
fix a man who's broke. There isn't enough
money in the world to do that. In the Bible
it says Ham was one of the three sons of Noah.
And that the Ark carried the last life
of the world for forty days and nights,
before resting on Mount Ararat.
A bus is like that, it can take you
rocking, leaning into bends of roads,
traveling home and away
and back again.

58

SANTA CRUZ

There's an old smell here,
creosote and steamed hot dog,
a mixture of fish head and scented candle;
the good stench of well-used rides.
The women here are mermaids,
watery. They move, no, syncopate
to all the sounds around, the dips and waves.
The men are Jeffers and Kerouacs, serious,
good-type-ers and foot tappers. There's
a wax museum feel to the horses
on the merry-go-round and the arcade
has an old-maid fortune teller
and new games with unfathomable rules.
It's hard to tell who's winning and who's
being electrocuted. I'm sucking down
a bitter micro-brew and the sky is turning
papery and crumpled, the lights on
the attractions bring down the space.
I like it. The soot of salt, the slush
of carnival music. Someone powers
a lead puck up the scale to he-man.
My head falls back. I wait for the sound
coming off the strike of the red bell.

AN OFFERING

I lean on the latitudes, the fixed.
Rely on equator, tropics of Cancer
and Capricorn. It's a search for
permanence, said Magellan—
the proof of a strange infinity
to circle all our lives— steadfast
in faith, the undulating seas like
bodies of love. And what about
the heavens, nameless winds
riding time. I can't fathom
mutterings, musings. Only things
locked in the moment, only
the healing touch. As I would
coax a bird to eat wild seed
from my outstretched hand.

ROME

Everything is as intricate as faith, as biting,
everything entwined, like love, like desire.
Two monks walk arm-in-arm across the Piazza Del Sol
into dark, into a catacomb; under autumn's full moon,
the slapping sound of their sandals.
The sound of a Vespa whining through the narrow
   streets.
The sound of a man alone as Adam on the fifth day,
the sound of him pissing off a balcony into the night.
The cry of a woman moving to her lover's touch, the
   echoes.
I lie in bed straining to my rhythms of loneliness,
waiting for the sun to burn away the quiet noise,
waiting for the sun to fill the day like red wine in a
   green bottle,
pushing till there's no room left against the heavy night.

GREAT FIRES

Before Nero set fire to the city,
before he had his wife and mother murdered,
in the good days, when he was a young man
and the oracles had predicted
he would live well into his eighties;
Nero rode his royal carriage
through the streets of Rome,
vestal virgins sprinkling his path with flowers,
(the emperor notoriously fond of flowers),
a centurion following with a legion of soldiers
past the cheering crowds.

The Renaissance fresco of this affair survives.
You enter it with your eyes, study the exuberant
faces attending, his imperial hand
holding a lily to his nose, the road
ahead petaled, fading into chips
and cracks of peeling pigment.
Here then is what you see,
a triumphal song left unfinished,
art that strikes at the heart.
It is like love and death.
Filled with flowers and great fires.

A DIMENSION OF LIGHT AND PARTICLES

Pygmies see everything as flat,
linear, as even with the landscape.

They see themselves as equal
with the sky, the sky equal with the land

as we would perceive a horizon as one line
meeting one line. They have no language

of their own yet they have 1000 words
for wind: three are translatable—

feather, heart and breath.
For them there are two true colors:

light and dark, and they are the same.
They can sing you three songs

and there will be cranes in all of them.
They tap sticks on hollowed

trunks of baobab trees; the sound
rhyming with the grain that is no longer.

Everywhere they exist adds dimension
to existing light. They say where light

meets other light is limbo, where earth
meets earth, purgatorial. They say there is no hell,

only a heaven where light meets land,
where one dimension becomes another.

PSALMS AND NUMBERS

Adam does not know what reasoning is
just yet, right now it's God and the garden—
a perfect day in paradise. Has it been almost a week?
he thinks. Tries to make sense of flowers,
fruits, roots gone aerial— was that a hiss?
and then he meets the girl of his dreams,
he likes hanging out with her, understands
now the missing parts, what he couldn't quite
put his finger on— God gone off resting.
Now here's the tricky part, placing blame.
Even angels know it takes two
to dance a tango on a head of a pin.
Maybe there is more than one snake—
behind every branch, under every rock.
Sometimes God is just inadequate,
not up to the job. Leaves it up to the tenants
to figure out the rules. Like a word jumble,
Eden could be Need.
Living rent free has its drawbacks.
Better to stay in a lean-to, spend the day
at the Jordan, a few quick dips.
Adam looks through the cracks
of the palm-frond shack,
sees the sun divided between the invisible,
the visible, has the best thought
he's had in a fortnight; he likes this woman Eve,
a lot. Digs being with her.
Never cared much for leisure anyway.
Book 1, Chapter 1, they start
their story of creation.

I AM WHO I AM

When Jesus was asked the question,
who are you? this was his answer,
loosely translated. The question being
are you the one who is prophesied.
I like the way a line can be indirect....

When the man who won reprieve
from the death sentence was asked
what will you do now? he answered,
breathe a little easier. A life sentence
all of a sudden is a breath let out in a whoosh.

To live is to have choices.

What will I do today?
Today I watch the landscape;
that ridge over there, where
the solid curve of line becomes
the thigh of some god, a reclining Buddha
turning inward, the way a good answer
turns back onto itself: Am I? Who am I?

I WANT TO FEEL

the tremble of a salmon
as it fights its way
up the river,
as the river
feels its way
from the mountain,
the slow melt
of snow. I want
to feel as Adam
must have felt
the first day
when he saw Eve,
her arm raised,
fingers extended.
To be there when
she turned
the first time
to look at him.
Feel the wind
over her nakedness,
see in the palm
of her hand
a single seed,
the knowledge
of what it is
to feel.

RETURNING

VENTS

I stand on the redwood deck,
        night caving last light,
boards pinging with release;

        the metal deck-clips cooling.
Charcoal in the old Weber
        sizzles from drops of chicken fat.

Vents closed, the coals blacken
        like tonight, the stars retracted.
It's the black holes I'm thinking of,

        a human body caught in their pull
would snap in two, each receding
        segment snap further in two,

compressed and collapsed.
        A whole sun reduced
to the size of a dot on a page,

        total implosion, then release.
New creation from old. Air chills around my insteps.
        Bay trees on the downslope

inch in view, sinister in their wind-wave.
        I'm struck between the urge
to go farther and the urge
        to return inward.

WHAT THE STARS SAY

I don't ask them the big questions.

They speak like wishes come true, eternal
covenants shooting clean through

at whatever is desired. They are
the only world I know outside my own.

It is too little.

Because I know what they say, over and over
is nothing, and forever

the same. Parallel lines cross no matter what.
What never changes?   Nothing.

What changes?   Everything.

WOLF IN THE FOLD

I'm half awake. Bells from St. Rita's
clanging down to ground,
as if they fell from the belfry, rolled
in semi circles on Sir Francis Drake Blvd.,
the clappers, languishing tongues; the old
religion dead. Hasn't anyone heard,
god moved to lower case.
The insignificant puffing in the sky, Olympians
going nowhere, just resting.
I gauge time by cloud movement,
some days like today, stationary in the breathless.
A cloud year, rotations in slow motion or whirlwind
weather change, the church quiet,
the Messiah safe behind leaded glass.
A chainsaw buzzes in and out,
bellies on the valley floor and rises up the hills,
groaning. The tree falls
opening a hole in the heart, leaving
in its place another hole to fill.
Cloud time gathers at the ridge, ready
to spill over. The church roof leaks dust;
it's all smoke and swords.
Sound travels. The clouds
take their time trolling.

REPAIR

It is a good day, the wind
neither too easterly nor too westerly,
and I'm repairing a loose board
on the apron of my garage, something put off
for at least a year. And now my neighbor
Mike Di Carza comes by, eager
to talk, to help. He has a cat claw
in hand, a tool to grab the ungraspable.
I show him the deck nails I'm using,
galvanized aluminum, and the saved
piece of clear-heart redwood to replace
the wornout, split board. And somehow
he talks about crows, how they pick
up gum wrappers and shiny bits of metal,
how they gravitate and deposit their find
into vents coming out of the tar and gravel
roofs common in our neighborhood.
His gout is bad today but he gets down
on knee and haunch to show me
how to use the claw of a hammer
to straighten a nail, suggests I drill
pilot holes, tosses the old and rusted nails
over the fence, where they burrow in the oak
leaves on the downslope and wait.

TO GET THERE

The name of the next town is Woodacre,
and the next San Geronimo, then Lagunitas,
then Olema. Make a left onto Limantour Road
to the beaches, slow down as you approach the curve,
the small creek funneled under the roadbed.
Stop and pick raspberries, take care you don't
get ripped by the razor-sharp thorns. Don't try
to save any berries, eat them right there. Notice the dark
under the trees, the madrone and bay, the pine
and valley oak. Take the next left and go about
a quarter of a mile to the first pullout along
a grassy field busy with birds. Look back
over the hill you've traveled, and if there's a need,
take a pee out in the open. Listen
to the chirp and whir of locust, feel the sun hot
on your back, the wind whipping your hair.
Continue on for about 8 miles; watch
for elk herds, wild turkey. When you get
to the parking lot you'll notice how the interior
of your car seems repressive; it's the ocean,
the pour of seawater through the slough
of the tide pools. Push the door against the stiff
winds and walk the next one thousand feet
to the tawny sand; take note of the terns, the ravens
sitting in the dead cypress, the insistent flies
on stranded sea grass. You have the whole day
to yourself. There is no next town, nowhere to go.

SWITCHBACK

The switchback climbed
the stubbled hill,
terraced its way around.
Even from the valley
we could see
people with their hands
on their hips;
shadowy figures
near leafless trees.
We drove on, passed
through a redwood park,
through showers
of yellow-brown needles,
and pendulous forms
bowing like butlers.
At Point Reyes Lighthouse
we could see elk herds
from the bluff.
Last year a jogger
was killed near here
by a mountain lion.
The mother
and her cubs tracked down.
Hunters in orange parkas
tied their bodies
on poles, carried
them out swaying,
the raw sea wind
at their backs.
We pulled our scarves
close up
under our chins
for warmth.

THE GARAGE

The recycling bins are filled, their capacity
to hold what can change into something
new and usable waits to be returned.
In another corner, a plastic nativity scene:
The baby Jesus asleep in a cradle
of excelsior, the donkey and lamb looking
dumbly on, Joseph carving a rocking horse
in his head, and Mary, a light on her face,
attending her son. Layers of dust, pollen, soot.
The driver backs the car out, the garage
door unfolds to a box of concealment.
The tar and gravel roof soak up the day's heat,
fennel sways in the breeze. Everything
empties, waiting to be refilled.

THE BUILDERS

It is July, the sun is wearing
a yellow jacket and the flowers
in my garden don't look confused
for once, they're soaking in energy,
opening up and smell just fine.
Hanging in a bramble of acacia
is a nest of wasps, a spun globe
of saliva and fiber; one hole near
the bottom for entry— there's no traffic
today because yesterday I soaked it
with poison from a safe distance.
I feel terrible. But they can drop a horse,
if the horse is tied to a post and rail,
in less than an hour. What's a man
compared to a horse? fifteen minutes?
And I was warned that if they come at you,
you should run to shade because
the dark confuses them. Yes, there's
commonality among the living.
Towards dusk I'll go near the hive
again, cut it free with long loppers,
show it to neighbors, slice it open
to a wake of bodies stacked neatly
around the queen.

HOW TO MAKE A SCARECROW

You'll need two branches from an oak, fresh cut,
green, resilient, sturdy enough to take the wind.
One long, stout, maybe five feet tall,
the other shorter, like a man holding out his arms
for a field sobriety test or a joke about Jesus.

You'll need a plaid flannel workshirt,
something with yellow in it or bright red,
color of the intestines of a fresh slaughtered pig.
And dungarees— faded, patched, quiltlike on the knees, _
the stitches crossed, irregular— and a bandana
like the one in John Wayne's hip pocket

blue with white stars, for a face with too many eyes,
and a hat like Huck Finn would wear.
You'll need to stuff the legs and arms with straw,
'til they have the feel of bones in a dead squirrel,
fill the chest cavity with rags, the head with dried leaves.

Just remember, from their roost in leafless trees
crows connive to steal the young
of other birds, to take them by the throat;
think of ways to beat you, get at what's yours.
With rags, mementos, with the long-used,
we try to save the things we love.

LESSEN

Straw bones rest in the field. The smell
of ripeness feeds, the tilled earth turned
to mud. A tattered feather in the muck;
the body it came from, off to nothing.
The day both cold and wet, little difference
between. And the wind, louder
without rows of corn. The scarecrow, alone
in a milliner's hat, waits in the decrease,
and off in the distance, ...pawh... pawh...
The sound of a shotgun.

WATCHING THE CORN

Some of the ears have been picked at,
a few sweet kernels plucked by crows
who don't heed me. I am a presence
in the cornfield, protector of the
farmer's crop. I can't exactly feel
anything, not having the sense
I was born with; old clothes, the mulch
of discards. Still, when the wind picks
up the tatters of my shirt sleeves,
the straw in my neck whistles, I come
alive, and the feeders flee to high
tension wires, hide under the barn's
eaves. I take satisfaction in being,
pleasure at the possibility to scare.
Yesterday the farmer's boy came,
mashed his cigarette out in my vacant eye,
left the cork-tipped filter in my socket
and hissed, out loud, how he'd set me
afire after the harvest on mischief night.
Something stirred my arm, swung
at his sternum. He ran back
to his yellow house. And a mouse
squeaked through my straw fingers.
Puppeteer, fearless scout from a brood.
Sometimes I swear I can hear
the corn grow, smell the ripening
on a breeze.

AN ATTENDANT'S TALE

My neighbor has a cat he swears
is the best ratter in Marin County.
He swears she is the reincarnation of Aphrodite.
Look at the way she sashays, he says, and the way
she attends her place on my aggregate stoop.
He says each morning he finds a rat;
sometimes chewed at the neck
or dead without a scratch or sometimes just a tail.
It's hard to argue with claims
to the rights of something no one wants.
I catch sight of a crow ravishing
an unguarded nest of warblers.
What are the rights and wrongs of anything?
Do you remember the cartoon in the funny papers:
a dog waiting behind the open door of a clothes dryer
as a cat approaches to investigate
the fandango of shirt sleeves and pant legs,
enticing her to hop in for a spin.
The dog, a long-nosed beagle is saying
in the caption, "please, please..."
I'm thinking of Aphrodite springing
from the foam of the sea
and I'm watching a spider embroider a web
to snare some oak moth or whitefly
so she can feed her young,
except she has no young.

STAYING PUT

I'm climbing an old apple tree, limbs
changing course where branches
have been left growing anywhere
the sun takes them, the hard fruit shaded
red and green, a traffic light for bees
humming through, the smell of pectin
dissolving. Sunlight shatters here
and there between the trembling
leaves as I scrape a leg in a crutch of bark,
then steady my footing, reach
a horizontal rung to rest an arm.
Despite the false arrangement I feel
in control, though disarmed. My lips
parting with verbs: to feather, to perfume,
to smell, to snake my tongue over
unblemished skin, to bite an apple
turned sweet, to stay here as if
free to do this, all summer, into fall.

MID-NOVEMBER

Floating overhead, a lone hawk
circling higher, each measure matching
the above with the less below.
A cold duty, this patrol of the weakened,
the unaware. It's been too long
since I last sought out the ocean, and today
I start out on the winding drive.
Anticipation guides the wheel, turns this way
inward, leading to a greater
outward turn; an escape from what holds,
land and land's end,
the pull-away of betweens. Unpredictable.
What lifts can also lower;
the chance-taking the sea offers.
Just as the hawk, farther from the prey
increases territory, decreases
survival. Too close as dangerous as too far.
It cuts both ways.

UNDERSTORY

Snow covers the ground and my steps
crunch the understory; the tight-packed
leaves, a dead bird perhaps, the warming
of trillium, birthroot waiting for thaw.
On either side, bare trees, a view
of white birch bark with black cut marks
and stands of somber-rilled chestnut oaks.
The only green is the mountain laurel.
Smoke drifts low from the singe of wood
I cannot see; it is there I am headed,
my eyelids stiff from the cold, my chin
numb, breath forming ghosts before me;
and the only sound is in me, muffled,
contained. As I come into the clearing,
new snow starts falling, powdery, so that
vision blurs and at the corners, doubles.
And for a second nothing makes sense—
a burned-out campfire smolders, four
hooves arranged in a square dance,
a head with two gaping holes where
the antlers are twisted off. It is as though
I've come upon the underworld.

SOUTH JERSEY

Whoever says you can't
go home again is wrong.
Basking in late spring blooms,
gorging on salt-water taffy.
Sure there are differences, more
signs, warnings, and the beach
grasses have been replanted
after a fifty year hiatus.
I'm just old enough to know
both ends of change.
High season not in full swing,
I walk the low-tide shore picking up
seashells and bits of sea glass.
A three-foot-long sand shark
grounded at the edge, eyes missing,
winks with intake of surf water.
I toe it over, white belly and mouth
frown, turn it back, make repair.
Flying above, laughing gulls.
Wind pushing and pulling.
Head down in wind-force, returned
to do what I've always done,
move from here to here.

RETURN

Rock exposed. The sea controls,
a restless blue waste, eating away,
making new land fall, etch of harbor.
Ultimately the feeding creates a woman
lying on her side; she turns to longing,
then distress. A Siren's call? And men come
weary from the long sail to rest
on her shore, the hollow sound
strangely pleasing. Forgetting themselves
is the beginning, the conjoining. Nothing
can be wrested from the sea, and rock-lined
faults, fissures, held by flanks, sigh.

NIGHTDAY

A friend with AIDS visits me.
                    It is the grainy time.
He and his boyfriend are off to the movies, revivals
                              of film noir.
It's mid-February,
          shortest month that's always longest
for me, and I'm left
              to reflect, drink
a glass of red, turn the rheostat up,
                    sharpen
my pen and struggle some words
                    on the page,
ink it up, read aloud.
              So much for erasures.
The impossible, the indelible
              is the pattern.
All the stale
        thoughts surge back
                  to when television
was an infant resting
            in the wee hours,
and not until
          the cracks of light, the old metaphors
seeped at
        the sash, around the doorjamb,
did anyone rise.
              What ever happened to...
How long the dead, dead...
                  But I restart;
free myself of paper and construction,
                  throw on a long overcoat,
walk beside blackened
          streets, survey odd angles,
old grids. Trees silent
            with birds, leaves knifing

ancient light; stars from
                the bitter past,
moon still envious.
           The play's an aside,
and so I turn,
          not exactly a new leaf,
but toward the neon downtown.
               Plaster my face back on.
A mask is a mask.
          Ask Janus the two-timer.
Rejoin the living,
        the ones who know
            no better.

REMEMBRANCE

I have listened.
The sound of water is never the same.
I have tried to learn
the sound by heart. I have tried to learn
by heart a river
sound, a sea, a drenching rain
that drowns the dog
day of summer, a soft drizzle. Anything
to do with water
never sounds the same. I have tried
to learn by heart
the name of water. The name of water
is never the same.
The spelling of water is ever changing,
the way the mouth
forms the word holds the change.
Two hands cupped
under a faucet, two hands held
high above
the leaping waves. One tear clinging.
One swept away.
The sound of water is never the same
and that is how I
remember. The name is never the same
and that is how
I lock it away, unlock the sound.

FOG

A voice from behind asks,
what are you thinking, and I start
to turn, realize the voice was mine
speaking aloud on this cliff at Land's End,
the Pacific blue and flaring, from up here
making hushing sounds.
A penny for your thoughts, I say,
talking to myself again. Really I wasn't
thinking at all, I'd reached that place
where body disappears and
the mind's freed, just being, carried
away, lifted from the conscious.
A tern makes a pass across my view
into a band of sunlight and for a while
nothing exists, except the light
and the polish of fog
touching everything.

ABOUT THE AUTHOR

Joseph Zaccardi was born in Newark, New Jersey.
He went to Catholic school through the ninth grade,
and then transferred to Sayreville War Memorial High
School. After graduation, he enlisted in the Navy,
served three years in Vietnam. He moved to San
Francisco in 1970 and worked as a barber and hair
stylist. Since 1987, he has resided in Fairfax, California.
His poems have appeared in: The Baltimore Review,
Blue Unicorn, Poet Lore, Runes, The Seattle Review
and elsewhere. He was a recipient of the Individual
Artist Grant from the Marin Arts Council in 2003.